Escape from Alcatraz

True Stories of Jail

Breaks and Great

Escapes

Roger Harrington

Table of Contents

How To Escape From Alcatraz : Jail Breaks

In 1621, a Dutch writer named Hugo Grotius was banished to a place named Loevestein Castle in the Netherlands; a location which served as a jail for political prisoners. Throughout his imprisonment, Grotius noted that a box in his cell was regularly removed, re-filled with books and then returned to his jail cell.

On 22nd March 1621, Grotius devised a plan with an accomplice inside the same jail. He would hide himself in the box, the guards would take the box to the library with him inside, and then Grotius would subtlety escape.

It worked. Grotius then fled the Netherlands and never returned.

What little information we know about the simple-but-ingenious escape plan hatched by Hugo Grotius forms the basis of every subsequent prison break which has followed right up until the present day. Despite its simple execution, it required creativity and cunning in equal parts. It required the assistance of an outside force and it required both mental and physical preparation. When the time came, it also required a sledge-hammer approach to escaping. In Grotius's case, it was to simply flee as fast as possible.

While the Grotius case may be the earliest jail break in recorded history, there has been no shortage of similar tales which have followed in the ensuing centuries. Prison breaks are a staple of modern popular culture, meaning they have been with us for at least 400 years.

Over time, the sheer amount of methods which prisoners have devised in order to escape confinement tally into the hundreds. Some methods are tried-and-tested and could potentially work under multiple different circumstances, whereas some methods are devised purposely for the situations which prisoners may find themselves in.

Jail-break methods such as applying sheer force to walls, doors and windows may be the most common type of escape employed across the world. Applying pressure to walls in order to create a tunnel has been used for centuries, and is commonly known today thanks to the 1994 movie the Shawshank Redemption. Other methods of escape involve more deceitful tactics, such as feigning illness in order to access areas otherwise restricted to prisoners, or exploiting the corrupt agendas of prison staff or law enforcement officials.

While jail breaks may seem like they're occurring more commonly than ever, statistics from 2013 show the rate of prison escapes have gradually decreased over the past twenty years. The actual figure of how many people escape from prisons each year is difficult to ascertain due to the legal implication of what qualifies as an 'escape'.

In the eyes of the general public, a prison escape is usually regarded as a high-profile, complex scheme devised by multiple individuals inside a high-security unit, usually involving tunneling through walls or breaking through ventilation shafts. While these kinds of breaks do happen on occasion, they are incredibly rare.

A more common 'escape' is for an inmate to simply walk out of a prison and never return. Many offenders are admitted to 'open' jails which don't require an offender to spend all of their time in prison. They are free to go to their place of employment or partake in community service. This is where the majority of offenders 'escape' from, despite it not being the grandiose gesture we have to come associate with the term 'jail break'.

Of course, maximum security prisons are much harder to break free of, and much rarer to hear about. In the five-year span between 2009 and 2013, only one inmate escaped from a maximum-security prison, while nine escaped from minimum- or medium-security facilities. More importantly, however, is that all ten inmates were recaptured within 24 hours.

It is important to understand why inmates can escape prisons which are considered to be impenetrable. In the case of the some of the subjects in this volume, it is clear to say that some prisoners' creativity knows no boundaries. No matter the circumstances, a sufficiently-devious mind will find a way to break free.

Furthermore, the idea of an 'inescapable' facility can create determined attitudes from prisoners, as well as relaxed attitudes from prison staff. It is possible for guards to believe that the walls around them will do their job for them, which can lead to oversights, errors and complacency.

As with all negative occurrences, prison breaks can serve as lessons in how to stop such things happening over and over again. Whenever a jail break occurs, prison officials will take further security precautions to ensure no one is able to escape via the same manner. Many commonplace security measures across all prisons are in place because of escape attempts which forced officials to act accordingly.

Barbed wire and razor wire was not a staple of prisons until the early 1900s after hundreds of escape attempts forced jails to put precautions in place. The same can be said of bars between cell windows, floodlights highlighting the surrounding area, and routine head counts of prisoners before lights out.

Despite their place in popular culture, jail breaks are an incredibly daring prospect for any criminal to undertake. In most countries, escaping from jail is a very serious offence and will certainly result in a harsher punishment once the subject has been re-captured. Depending on the severity of the crime for which the offender was originally imprisoned, an attempted jail break can result in a significantly longer sentence.

The cases covered in this volume are a combination of those prisoners who went to extreme lengths in order to free themselves from the confines of jail, those who broke free as a declaration of their innocence, and those who simply pounded at the first opportunity to escape. The fascination of each case cannot be over-stated, as well as the unimaginable bravery and audacity each one required.

The 1962 Alcatraz Escape

Alcatraz prison is synonymous with security. Even in modern language, the word 'Alcatraz' itself has come to be a metaphor for anywhere with intense security measures or a place of sheltered isolation. Alcatraz Island is located over a mile off the shore of San Francisco Bay in California. Before it was closed in 1963, it was considered to be the most secure prison facility in the world due to its solitude.

Attempting to escape from prison is risky enough without the added element of being located on a secluded island far from civilization, so to attempt an escape from Alcatraz would be considered by many to be a death wish.

On the night of June 11th 1962, three inmates inside Alcatraz Federal Penitentiary would pull off the impossible. They would escape the inescapable.

Prisoners Clarence Anglin, John Anglin and Frank Morris would break out of Alcatraz, cross the 1.25 miles of harsh waters of the San Francisco Bay and escape to a life they thought they would never see again.

Every escape plan needs a mastermind, and the 1962 Alcatraz escape had Frank Lee Morris. Morris has since been portrayed in the movie "Escape from Alcatraz" as an ingenious criminal with a brain designed for deception; and this as close to reality as a portrayal can come.

Morris had grown up with a somewhat-clichéd criminal background. He was admitted to multiple foster homes growing up due to neglectful parents. His first crime would come at the age of thirteen for thievery, and his subsequent teenage years saw him progress from stealing to drug possession to armed robbery; racking up an impressive resume of different crimes.

As the severity of Morris' crimes escalated, so did his prison sentences. By his late twenties he was a regularly in and out of different jails, culminating in a 10-year prison sentence at Louisiana State Penitentiary. Morris, true to his future infamy, would escape from Louisiana. He would be captured less than a year later, and was deferred to the inescapable Alcatraz.

Prison officials would later credit Morris with possessing genius-level intelligence. He had an IQ of 133 and was considered to be in the top 2% of the general population regarding his intellect. It is not surprising that, in the entire history of Alcatraz Federal Penitentiary, he was the only one to mastermind a successful escape.

Although Morris was the perpetrator of the escape, two other inmates would join him on the journey. Brothers John and Clarence Anglin were serving time at Alcatraz for armed robbery, and three had become acquainted during a previous stint they all endured at Atlanta State Penitentiary some years prior. All three men were lifelong criminals with vast credentials of prison sentences, robberies and even jail breaks to their names. Together, the three would go down in history as real-life criminal masterminds

The scheme began to form in December 1961, six months prior to the event. An inmate named Allen West – who assisted in the jail break but was unable to escape himself – discovered a set of saw blades which appeared to have been discarded by prison maintenance staff. Allen hid the blades in his cell (although it is unclear where or how he managed to do this successfully for such a long period of time).

The plan – despite sounding simple on paper – involved some incredibly complex methods in order to execute it accordingly. The prisoners planned to saw through the ventilation grills in their cells which would lead to an un-guarded corridor, make their way to the outside of the prison through the windows of the facility, finally climbing down a kitchen ventilation pipe to freedom. There, they would use materials they had obtained inside the prison to create a makeshift boat to sail back to civilization.

Both Morris, the Anglin Brothers and Allen West (the unsuccessful escape attempter) occupied cells in close proximity to each other. The initial steps of the escape plan began by sawing away at the concrete surrounding the ventilation grills in each inmate's cell. Using the saws which West had obtained as well as homemade weapons made from various materials inside the jail, they would begin hacking away at the concrete around 5:30pm and continue until lights out.

After five months of sawing, Morris and the Anglin brothers had completely hollowed out their respective cells' six-by-nine inch ventilation grills. Each one led to the same area which presented ventilation they needed to see through. This one was significantly larger but was able to be chiseled away easily due to the combined efforts of all three men.

They would rotate shifts; one would work away at the ventilation shafts while one kept lookout for guards. As this was going on, the Anglin brothers began working on their smoking gun – dummy replicas of their heads.

These dummy heads, while appearing lifelike from a distance, were an obvious forgery on closer look. The Anglin brothers created them homemade cement-powder mixture and toilet paper. They were painted to resemble the features of the brothers and Morris, even incorporating human hair which the group had stolen from the floor of the prison barbershop.

The amount of materials which the inmates obtained from inside the prison is nothing short of remarkable. In order to craft the required items to cross the 1.25 miles of ocean between Alcatraz and the mainland, they stole fifty raincoats which they turned into life jackets and a raft large enough to hold all of them. In order to bind the materials for their requirements, they stitched them together and used the heat from the steam pipes behind their cells to forge them. For their paddles they stole pieces of wood from around the prison.

Each evening after their work was finished; they would exit through their ventilation grills and place their escape materials above their cells so there was small chance of the objects being discovered by guards. They would then return to their cells before continuing the process the following day.

They considered their makeshift raft to be the biggest concern as inflating it by mouth alone would take a significant amount of time. In order to rectify this, Morris stole a musical instrument similar to an accordion known as a concertina. The air flow it was possible to create allowed them to inflate the raft at a much quicker rate than they could manually, allowing them the possibility of a quicker escape.

After lights out on June 11th 1962, the group felt it was time to make their escape.

At around 9:30pm, Morris obtained the dummy heads from above their cells and informed the group that they would be attempting their liberation that evening. There was no planned date in place for their escape; it was simply down to whenever they were fully prepared.

Unfortunately, Allen West was unable to remove the ventilation grate from his cell. He was planned to be the fourth escapee but the group had to leave him behind due to an error in his planning. West had used cement to re-seal the hole so as not to raise the suspicions of prison guards. However, the cement had gradually hardened and was now unable to break it in such a short amount of time.

The group planted the dummy heads in their beds in order to fool guards into believing they were sleeping. Morris and the Anglin brothers then made their way into the utility corridor behind their cells, and there they made their way onto the prison roof.

They maneuvered across the roof and down a pipe to the prison courtyard. They then climbed two 12-foot barbed-wire fences to the northeast shoreline and used the concertina to inflate their makeshift raft. They then headed towards Angel Island, around two miles in the distance.

It would be the last known movement of Frank Morris, Clarence Anglin and John Anglin. To this day, they have not been seen since.

What happened to the escapees after this night is widely speculated. For years, authorities believed that the group most likely drowned in the San Francisco waters. Despite it being summertime and the waters being relatively calm, the fact they escaped in the midnight hours meant the waters would have been at their most harsh for the time of year. Regardless, there is circumstantial evidence which points to the group's plans both failing and succeeding.

When authorities became aware of the escape, Allen West was quick to explain the events to officers in order to relieve himself of any future punishments for being involved. West claimed that the men had planned to steal a car and burglarize a clothing store once they had reached the shore, but intense investigation yielded neither of these crimes being committed in the San Francisco area at the time they would have likely arrived on land.

While authorities stated it was entirely possible for the escapees to have reached Angel Island safely, they also claimed that the freezing midnight temperatures made it highly unlikely. Over the ensuing weeks, discarded items from the group washed up on the San Francisco shore. Amongst the items were the paddles which the group had used to sail their raft. A wallet belonging to one of the Anglin brothers (the information inside had details of the Anglin brothers' relatives). Some of the material used to fashion the raincoats which they wore as well as parts of their homemade raft.

Despite no bodies being discovered, it was the conclusion of many that the group had perished in the freezing waters. As of 1973, the official FBI investigation into the case has been closed with the result that the perpetrators "most likely drowned".

It wasn't until 1993 that former Alcatraz inmate Thomas Kent came forward with information that he was involved in the plan to escape with Morris and the Anglin brothers but refused to go through with it. Kent told authorities that Clarence Anglin's girlfriend was poised to meet them on land and drive the group to Mexico.

While it would have been difficult for the inmates to maintain contact with the outside world throughout their incarceration – particularly on such a regular basis and to such a necessary degree – it is not impossible given what they did manage to pull off.

Over the years, more and more people have come forward with information relating to the escape which gives weight to the belief that the group may have been successful in their escape. In 2011, a program for the

National Geographic Channel claims that footprints were discovered on Angel Island beach close to a wreckage of parts which could have been part of the escapee's raft. The program also claims that a car was stolen from nearby the beach, despite the official FBI report claiming the opposite.

The same year, a relative of Frank Morris claimed that he had personally taken a multitude of envelopes to Alcatraz guards while they were off-duty. Bud Morris, Frank Morris's cousin, was unsure himself as to why he was asked to pass the envelopes on, but did so at the request of his cousin. He soon realized that they were likely bribes so that guards would look the other way.

This claim does indeed hold weight, as on

the night of the inmates' escape, a loud bang was reportedly heard at around 10pm. This was likely the large ventilation grill in the un-guarded corridor falling to the ground, yet this was not investigating by any of the on-duty prison guards. It seems unlikely that such a loud disturbance would not generate immediate attention from officials.

The sisters of the Anglin brothers have since claimed that they fully believe their brothers to be alive as they have received brief contact from them over the years. One of the sisters said that she received a phone call from John Anglin shortly after their 1962 escape, but she was unwilling to make this public knowledge for fear of legal repercussion. The same year, the Anglin brothers' mother received a Christmas card saying: "To

Mother, from John. Merry Christmas".

The Anglin brothers reportedly sent cards to family members for several years following their escape. In 2015, these cards were presented to authorities for handwriting analysis in order to determine if they were genuine.

Although there were no dates on the cards, the family members who received them were adamant they were received post-1962. The handwriting analysis was a match, confirming that the cards were indeed written by the Anglin brothers.

Perhaps the most interesting piece of evidence comes in the form of photograph provided by an Anglin family friend. Fred

Brizzi, who was childhood and teenage friends with both of the brothers claimed that he saw both of them working on a farm in Rio de Janeiro in 1975. It is unclear why Brizzi had taken a photograph of the men, or indeed why they would allow him to do such a thing given their status as wanted fugitives, but the men in the photograph did indeed bear an incredible resemblance to both brothers. The photograph, when passed to authorities, was proven to have been taken in 1975, 13 years after their escape. The official conclusion was that the men in the photograph were "most likely" the Alcatraz escapees.

The Alcatraz 1962 escape is a classic mystery; no doubt the greatest prison break mystery of all time. The escape required six months of intense planning which had to be followed to the letter. There were rumors of others being involved in the escape, but Frank Morris was unwilling to let them be a part of it due to the risk presented by having too many people involved.

Whether the group's plan was a failure or a success, there is no denying the incredible determination it requires to escape an inescapable fortress in the middle of a lake. Frank Morris and the Anglin brothers will go down in history as the only people to have ever achieved such a remarkable feat of endurance, perseverance and audacity.

Alfred Hinds – The Real Life Harry Houdini

The famous magician Harry Houdini once made the claim that he could unlock any door in the world. Indeed, Houdini was able to prove this claim time and time again. In the early 1900s, he regularly unlocked prison cell doors and padlocks with relative ease. He escaped from Murderers' Row in a Washington D.C. prison which houses some of the most violent criminals in the world. In Boston City Prison, Houdini escaped handcuffs, a prison cell, scaled the jail walls and ran a mile all within twenty minutes.

Despite his reputation as the world's greatest magician, Harry Houdini was simply a normal human with knowledge and skills with many others didn't possess. Luckily, Houdini used his skills for magic; art and entertainment. In the hands of a more devious mind, these skills could be used for much more deceptive reasons.

Enter Alfred Hinds, considered by many to be the criminal equivalent of Harry Houdini.

Alfred George Hinds is one of the celebrated prison escapees in history. Over his tenuous criminal career, Hinds managed to escape from a total of three high-security prisons throughout England, all in an attempt to show that he was an innocent man.

Born in London, England in 1917, Alfred Hinds suffered a traumatic upbringing. At a young age, Hinds' lost his father due to a severe bout of corporal punishment which he received as a repercussion for armed robbery. His father was given ten lashes from a cat o' 6 (the early 1900s equivalent of a cat o' nine tails), which rendered his body unable to cope with the severe pain, resulting in his death. This forced Hinds to turn to a life of crime to cope.

Following his father's death, Hinds was placed into a foster home in the London area. His difficult behavior would result in his attendance at regular foster homes in an incredibly short space of time; eventually seeing him at Pentonville Remand Home. This is where Hinds would make his first ever escape.

At the age of seven, Hinds ran away. Despite

his young age, he somehow managed to survive on the streets of London for several years before escaping to the West Midlands. It is believed that he found foster parents in the Midlands and took up learning metalwork and machine operations.

By the time of the Second World War, Hinds joined the Royal Tank Corps, although he eventually deserted them. Hinds arranged for accomplices to create a distraction while Hinds was being transported in an Army truck through the London area. When the guards were sufficiently distracted, Hinds escaped in a vehicle provided by another accomplice. A pattern of desertion was beginning to form in Hinds' life.

Eventually, Hinds was caught and

imprisoned for petty theft after resorting to a life of crime after his desertion from the military. He was sentenced to Rochester Borstal in 1945, which would come to be the first institution he would escape from.

It wouldn't be until September 1953 when Hinds' found him in serious trouble with the law. Hinds, along with four accomplices, were caught stealing around £30,000 worth of jewelry as well as around £5000 in cash from a Maple's store on a London high street. In 2017, this would be the equivalent around £250,000. Three months later, Hinds was sentenced to twelve years in Nottingham Prison.

It took the jury only thirty minutes to decide on the verdict of Alfred Hinds, despite there being very little physical evidence to tie him to the crime. The only evidence the jury had was circumstantial, but it was more than enough to convince them that Hinds was a guilty man. The prosecution claimed that traces of the materials which the robbers used to blow open the safe inside the jeweler store was discovered on Hinds' palms, along with actual residue from the blast itself.

In addition, Hinds had previous convictions of safe-breaking, so it was not a stretch to assume he played a significant role in the robbery.

Throughout his whole ordeal, Hinds maintained that he was an innocent man. In recent years he had shown signs of improvement and claimed that illegal activity was no longer part of his life. He was living with his brother in Staines and even worked for him as part of his construction business. Until the day he died, Hinds maintained his innocence.

He appealed his verdict instantly, but was dismissed on the grounds of a lack of alibi to determine his whereabouts on the night of the robbery. Hinds then published a pamphlet in which he demanded a retrial; however, his pleas were ignored by authorities. After two years of struggling to get anyone to pay attention to his ordeal, Alfred Hinds decided to escape from Nottingham Prison.

Hinds somehow obtained a hacksaw inside the prison; likely stolen from a maintenance worker or from a construction workshop. He used the hacksaw to fashion planks of wood which Hinds would use as a ramp to scale the prison walls. And in a move which wouldn't be out of place in Harry Houdini's repertoire of tricks, Hinds also memorized the shape of the key which opened his jail cell, and somehow made a copy of this key out of brass. In November 1955, Alfred Hinds escaped from Nottingham Prison.

For 245 days, Hinds remained a fugitive. During his time on the run, Hinds endeavored to make the world aware that he had been wrongly imprisoned. He sent letters declaring his innocence to every British newspaper he could. Hinds wrote a letter to the Daily Herald (the predecessor to the Sun) declaring: *"I made this escape because it was the only way now left open to me in my fight to obtain justice. I am entirely innocent of the crime for which I was sentenced for twelve years."*

Unfortunately for Hinds, all of the letters he had sent were postmarked with SW1, the code for South-West London. Authorities traced his whereabouts from London to Dublin, where Hinds was finally re-captured on 31st July 1956. He had been living in a cottage which he bought out-right, possibly with the money he stole from the Maple's robbery in London. Despite his capture, the majority of the cash has never been discovered.

It soon became clear that Alfred Hinds was not just a master jail breaker; he was also fully-versed in all aspects of criminal law. Hinds acted as his own defense during trial for his prison break attempt, and successfully managed to convince the jury to drop the charges he would endure for escaping prison. Reports state that during this trial, the prosecuting judge even admitted that Hinds was knowledgeable in aspects of criminal law which even he wasn't familiar with.

Hinds only received an extra eleven days added on to his previous sentence, despite breaking from jail and making a mockery of the security at Nottingham Prison.

Hinds' next escape would not be from jail, but from the Law Courts. By this point, Hinds' used his vast knowledge of criminal law to argue a point regarding his arrest after he broke out of jail. Hinds claimed that his re-arrest was illegal and unsolicited, and so appeared before Queen's Bench Division to state his claim.

Whilst there, Hinds arranged for his accomplices to supply him with a padlock. During the court proceedings, Hinds asked to go to the bathroom and was escorted by two guards. The guards removed Hinds' handcuffs as they let him in, to which Hinds overpowered the guards and locked them in the bathroom with the smuggled padlock. Hinds escaped from the Law Courts to Fleet Street but was captured within five hours.

All demands for a re-trial went unheard as Alfred Hinds' deception was now becoming a focal point. The media had learnt of Hinds' ordeals and sympathized with his troubles. The general public believed him to be wrongly convicted and so offered support to him in any way they could. He was slowly becoming a celebrity due to his impressive ability to escape from confinement as well as his regular protests of innocence.

Hinds was then sentenced to Chelmsford prison. The authorities attempted to keep his whereabouts a secret so as not to draw unwanted attention from people who were willing to help Hinds escape yet again. Unfortunately, their wishes went unfulfilled, as less than a year later; Hinds would escape one final time.

Inside Chelmsford prison, Hinds fashioned a

key in a similar manner to his previous escape. The key led him to the prison bathhouse, then onto the prison rooftop and down onto the ground. He escaped into a waiting vehicle driven by an accomplice of his.

Hinds would evade capture for nearly two years. He again returned to Ireland where he assumed the identity of William Herbert Bishop, a second-hand car dealer. He would be re-captured in 1960 for possessing illegally-imported vehicles. A crime which saw him serves six months in Belfast prison.

During the two years in which he remained free, Hinds continued to protest his innocence, sending letters and raped recordings to newspapers, authorities and the media. Despite his persistence, Hinds' claims went unheard and was sentenced to a final six years in Parkhurst Prison for all of his previous misdemeanors.

In 1964, Hinds was released from prison under normal circumstances. He retired to Jersey where he set up his own business. Hinds soon gained celebrity status throughout Britain. His incredible feats of prison escape afforded him the image of an ambitious man who would stop at nothing to present the truth to the world. The fact he escaped three high-profile British prisons with relative ease was testament enough to his incredible skills, but he also spoke with authority on the subject of the English legal system.

Hinds soon became a much sought-after speaker in regards to criticizing English law. He published a semi-autobiographical book of his times behind bars under the title Contempt of Court, which also documented the failings of the English system which subjected him to what Hinds claims was unfair treatment.

In a final nod to his legacy, a final attempt to contain Alfred Hinds was made by the students of University of Westminster in 1967. Under the presence of a hazing ritual, Hinds was jokingly kidnapped by several students who took him to the basement room at their university. Unfortunately, students were no match for the incredible deception which Hinds was capable of. Hinds somehow managed to escape the basement, trap the students inside and turn the lock on them. He then left them in there and walked off into the night.

To this day it is unclear whether Alfred Hinds was responsible for the robbery of the Maple's store in London in 1953. The circumstantial evidence presented by the courts gives a solid indication that he was, however, there is no official evidence which ties him to it.

If Hinds was indeed part of the robbery and therefore guilty, it seems strange that he would continue to protest his innocence so adamantly. If further evidence ever surfaced that Hinds *was* definitely involved in the robbery, it would tarnish his name and reputation for good.

This is also in addition to the fact that he contacted newspapers while he was a fugitive on the run. Most criminals who escape prison go into hiding and take every precaution to make their whereabouts unknown to the rest of the world. If Hinds were guilty, it seems highly unlikely he would do this. Alfred Hinds, it seemed, was more interested in justice than protecting his anonymity.

Alfred Hinds died in January 1991 at the age of 74. He will go down in history as the greatest British escape artist who ever lived. It was around the time of Hinds' Nottingham escape in which the media and general public began referring to him as "Houdini Hinds", a name almost certainly deserved. If Houdini was alive to see Alfred

Hinds in action, he would no doubt be impressed with what he saw.

Alfréd Wetzler and Rudolf Vrba – Holocaust Heroes

Alfréd Israel Wetzler was born on 10th May
1918. He was a Slovak Jew who became one
of the most important confidantes in the
history of the Second World War. Alfréd
Wetzler is one of the few Jews to have seen
the horrors of the Aushwitz death camp and
live to tell the tale. The information he would
come to provide would be invaluable to the
Allies.

Alfréd Wetzler was born in the town of
Trnava, Slovokia where he worked as a
manual laborer up until the Second World
War. In 1942, at 25 years old, Wetzler was
dispatched to the Birkenau holding camp for
one month before eventually being sent to

Auschwitz, Hitler's largest death site. Whilst there, Wetzler discovered that a childhood friend of his – Rudolf Vrba – was also being subject to the same fate as he was.

Rudolf Vrba was born in 1924 in Topoľčany, Slovakia. Vrba was enlisted in the English military during his youth, but would soon be deported to a holding camp in Czechoslovakia for Jews awaiting further deportation to Nazi camps. Vrba first attempted to escape this holding camp by simply running away at the first available opportunity. Unfortunately, Vrba was quickly discovered and subsequently beaten by the guards for his actions.

In Aushwitz, both Wetzler and Vrba were designated to handling the luggage of deportees. Wetzler became stuck in this role for a while but Vrba would eventually progress to becoming a train registrar. This involved Vrba being able to wander around Auschwitz without intense supervision – something that would aid his and Wetzler's later escape.

Eventually, both Vrba and Wetzler were designated to watching over laborers who were tasked with expanding the camp, allowing both of them mild freedom around Auschwitz – something which the majority of Jews never received.

On April 7th 1944, Wetzler and Vrba planned their escape of the Nazi death facility. At this point, the Nazis were strengthening their hold all over Europe. Jews were being deported to Auschwitz, gassed and burnt in their thousands each day. There was a constant scent of burnt bodies across the entire camp. Both Wetzler and Vrba knew that if they didn't make their escape soon, the Nazis would no longer have much use for them and they would suffer the same fate as their less-lucky counterparts.

There had been many instances of prisoners attempting to escape Auschwitz in the past, but as far as historical record goes, the only escape officially documented is that of Wetzler and Vrba. There is rumored to be around 150 escapees in total; an incredibly insignificant figure given the sheer amount of prisoners who passed through the camp.

The repercussions for anyone caught even

planning to escape from the death camp resulted in an execution of a Nazi officer's choice. Often, they were publically hanged. Other times they were sent to the "dark cell", a series of small jail cells in the basement of block 11, known as the "death block" These small cells were entirely deprived of light and poorly ventilated. Prisoners would serve out the hours or days of their sentence in complete darkness, subsequently suffocating to death.

Additionally, a particularly tormenting punishment for would-be escapees was the "standing cell" – a phone booth-type jail cell where around four people would be locked in at once. It would be impossible to sit down or sleep and eventually the body would die from exhaustion.

In order to avoid a similar fate, Wetzler devised the plan of covering his and Vrba's body in gasoline and tobacco in order to mask their scent from the guard dogs. The two men made their way outside the main gate of Auschwitz and kept themselves hidden within a stockpile of wood. They rationed all the food and water they had with them in order to prolong their survival. They remained there for three days before moving on.

They eventually made their way out of the camp and into the surrounding countryside. The following morning, Nazi officials realized that the pair was missing when roll-call was taken. They immediately dispatched officers to hunt down the pair, but by this point, Wetzler and Vrba were well on their way to Czechoslovakia.

By the time Wetzler and Vrba escaped, the Nazis had replaced as many Polish people in the towns and villages in the Auschwitz area as they could with ethnic Germans who were unquestionably loyal to Hitler and his regime. Wetzler understood that he and Vrba needed to make it to the Czechoslovakian border on their own – asking for help from anyone could lead to their re-capture. It would be difficult to know who to trust in such a fiercely-divided region.

The pair tried to blend into the countryside, but they stood out from everyone else because their heads were shaven, their clothes were filthy and they smelled of gasoline and burnt corpses. The Nazis searched for them with sniffer dogs, as well as employing a vast amount of officers and military convoys to locate them.

Although they took every precaution they could to evade any kind of civilization on their way to their intended destination, the pair accidentally wondered into a German town. Fearing for the worst, Wetzler and Vrba made sure to only navigate the backstreets where there was little chance of German patrol officers discovering them.

Fortunately, despite their beliefs that all Polish people had been removed by the German forces, Wetzler and Vrba came across several Polish farmers and villagers who were eager to help escapees from the camp and strike a blow against the despised Nazi regime. They helped escaped prisoners and local underground organizations including the Home Army, Polish Socialist Party, and Peasant Battalions, who worked to aid the fugitives.

Although they were completely lost and relying mostly on luck to not get re-captured, the pair eventually knocked on the door of a nearby house they believed to be safe. A peasant woman answered the door who agreed to help them on. It was a stroke of good fortune that the woman was a Polish peasant and not a purposely-placed German officer. The pair slept safely at her home until the morning time when they would continue their journey to Czechoslovakia.

After a day's rest, Vrba and Wetzler continued on their journey. They were still not even halfway to the Slovakian border and moving quickly along they stumbled onto a woman tending her crops. At first she was quite suspicious of them, but she eventually introduced them to a friendly Polish farmer who agreed to take them to the border and show them a place to safely cross. The last part of their journey took them two days, but finally the farmer guided them to a clearing near the border. They waited for a German patrol to pass and then they slipped into Czechoslovakia

After three days of hiding in a pile of wood outside the most horrific location in human history, fifteen days of walking more than 85 miles through occupied Germany and

Poland, Wetzler and Vrba arrived at the Jewish Council headquarters in Zilina, Czechoslovakia on April 25, 1944.

Vrba described the inhuman brutality that he and Wetzler had witnessed at the death camp to the Jewish Council. Its members shook their heads in horrified disbelief. Resistance fighters knew that the Nazis had terrorized Jewish communities for years.

They knew that the Nazis deported Jews to concentration camps and they had heard that the conditions in the camps killed many people. But sending people to gas chambers and crematoriums? It was almost impossible to imagine industrialized, bureaucratic, assembly-line mass killings.

It appeared that the Jewish Council were sceptical of the men's claims, and so requested that Wetzler and Vrba prove their story. They asked Vrba for the names of people that had been alongside him at Auschwitz and then ran the names against the records of the Jews who had been deported from Czechoslovakia.

Fortunately, Vrba anticipated that his claims may be met with suspicion, and so he had memorized every transport arriving at Auschwitz, as well as the number of people on each method of transport and how many people were immediately sent directly for execution. The Jewish Council again could not fathom what they were being told. Wetzler and Vrba's words had altered their record book into an obituary page.

Eventually, the Jewish Council was convinced that what the two men were claiming was the absolute truth. The Council then asked them to dictate everything they could remember about Auschwitz and its Nazi operators. As Vrba vividly recalled the horrific details, he stressed that the nightmare wasn't over and that the Nazis had targeted the Jews of Hungary as their next victims, and in fact, the Nazi officers had already prepared Aushwitz for their arrival.

The testimony of the two Auschwitz escapees provided the foundation for a report describing the early history of Auschwitz and the events which occurred in Auschwitz from April 1942 to April 1944. This report came to be known as the Vrba-

Wetzler report, and remains one of the most influential documents in the grand scheme of World War II.

After the Vrba-Wetzler report had been translated, couriers and communications sent it to people that needed to know about it, including the Vatican, the Jewish Community in Switzerland and British and American representatives in Switzerland.

The Allies had known since November 1942 that Jews were being killed in their hundreds of thousands in Auschwitz, and The Vrba-Wetzler report was an early attempt to estimate the numbers and was the most detailed description of the gas chambers to that point. The publication of parts of the report in June 1944 is credited with helping to persuade the Hungarian regent, Miklós Horthy, to halt the deportation of that country's Jews to Auschwitz, which had been proceeding at a rate of 12,000 a day since May 1944.

The report contained a detailed description of the geography and management of the Aushwitz camps, the way in which prisoners were forced to carry out their daily activities, and the severe methods of death which most prisoners were eventually subjected to. It listed the transports that had arrived at Auschwitz since 1942, their place of origin, and the numbers "selected" for work or the gas chambers.

Once the details of the Vrba-Wetzler report were sufficiently circulated, the Nazis' secret became public knowledge. All of the major leaders across the world had confirmation that the Germans were slaughtering millions of Jews, and in turn, banded together to put a stop to their atrocities.

In hindsight, the actions of Rudolph Vrba and Alfréd Wetzler have been referred to as "the largest single rescue of Jews in the second World War". What makes the heroic tale of these two fearless jail-breakers even more inspiring is that their initial imprisonment was entirely unwarranted. They never committed any kind of criminal act or had a history of unnecessary violence. They were simply captives of a corrupt regime who took their fate into their own hands.

When the horrors of the Second World War ended, both men went to on become established in their respective fields as well as being hailed as heroes for the rest of their lives. Vrba went on to become a successful biochemist focusing on cancer research, and Wetzler lived a quiet life as an editor in Bratislava. Both men have since passed on, but their memory lives on in stories of their heroism.

John Dillinger, Master Escapist

There are many criminals whose names we recognize but often aren't familiar with the specifics of their crimes. Al Capone, the Kray Twins, Baby Face Nelson, Jesse James. We instantly register that these people are infamous violent offenders but their actions have become almost mythical; something otherworldly. John Dillinger is one of these names.

John Herbert Dillinger was born on June 22nd, 1903. His name would become synonymous with bank robberies, murder and all-round violent behavior. He was the leader of the Dillinger Gang, and perhaps the most notorious gangster of the early 1900s.

But perhaps Dillinger's most incredible skill was his ability to escape from jail.

As a child, Dillinger regularly committed petty theft. In 1924 he robbed a grocery store, and was subsequently caught and jailed. True to his future infamy, Dillinger escaped this jail – an early sight of his incredible manipulation and overpowering abilities.

Dillinger then headed to Chicago, Illinois, to put together one of the most organized and deadly bank robbing groups in history.

Dillinger's first notable jail-break came in May 1933 at Allen County Jail in Lima, Ohio. Dillinger had been imprisoned for multiple robberies in the Ohio area, taking a total of around $10,000. Upon a search of Dillinger's prison cell, authorities discovered a document which appeared to be a prison escape plan, but Dillinger told them it was simply fantasy.

In actual fact, the plan was a detailed guide to how Dillinger was going to escape Allen County Jail. Whilst inside, Dillinger had acquainted himself with six other men who were also serving sentences: Pete Pierpont, Russell Clark, Charles Makley, Ed Shouse, Harry Copeland, and John "Red" Hamilton. The plan included details of how these men would also escape alongside Dillinger.

Dillinger had planned for outside acquaintances to smuggle firearms into the jail and hand them to his six accomplices. The six accomplices then used the firearms to escape their cells, then came and freed Dillinger.

It was not the most skilled method of jail-breaking, nor was there any deceitful methods employed by the more intellectual prison escapees throughout history. However, John Dillinger lived his life obtaining what he wanted through sheer force. This was the only method he understood.

However, less than a year later, Dillinger would surprise the world by employing a method of escape which is still regarded as remarkable today.

March 3rd, 1934 would cement his reputation as not just the most feared gangster in the

Western world, but an intelligent mastermind capable of escaping a high-security prison. Dillinger had been apprehended by Indiana State Police due to his involvement in a bank robbery in Arizona, and so was placed in Crowne Point jail.

Exactly how John Dillinger managed to pull off what followed is still a mystery as far as the history books are concerned; however, we do know the basic details of what happened.

On the morning of Dillinger's imprisonment, he somehow secured a "gun". Many reports claim that this was a gun made entirely of wood which Dillinger had somehow fashioned in the short time he was locked away. Some believe it was a fake gun which Dillinger already had with him at the time of his arrest, and some believe it was a genuine firearm which police had mistakenly not taken from Dillinger.

Whether it was a wooden gun he carved himself, a wooden gun he had already obtained, or even a real gun which may or may not have been smuggled into him will never be known.

It was a local joke in Crown Point that even master magician Harry Houdini wouldn't be able to free him from the "inescapable" Crown Point prison, but Dillinger was in the process of doing exactly that.

At 9:00 o' clock in the morning, using the wooden gun, he began his methodical escape by locking up several trusties, a jail attendant, a deputy sheriff, and the prison warden - each time getting valuable information from them about the geography of the prison. Dillinger knew he couldn't go far with the firepower he had (as he may not have had any at all). So Dillinger commandeered the use of the deputy sheriff, Ernest Blunk.

Dillinger headed towards the warden's office where he took with him two Thompson sub-machine guns which he had taken from Blunk. Dillinger then marched back toward the cells, taking Blunk's weapons and Blunk himself as a hostage. Once back at the cells, he asked the prisoners there if any of them wanted to escape with him.

A young black man, Herbert Youngblood, awaiting trial for murder, elected to go and was so handed a machine gun by Dillinger. Two other inmates also accepted the invitation and the group headed towards to the rear of the prison where the garage was located. Once in the garage, the two would-be escapee inmates got cold feet and backed out, leaving Dillinger and Youngblood on their own.

Whilst in the garage, Dillinger captured an assortment of people including the jail cook, kitchen helpers, several more trusties, and the warden's mother-in-law. While Youngblood held the group at gunpoint,

Dillinger sought out a vehicle for the pair to escape in.

Dillinger asked garage mechanic Edward Saager which car was the fastest, and was told it was the vehicle belonging to a local Sheriff. After pulling the ignition wires from the other cars in the garage, Dillinger, Youngblood, deputy sheriff Blunk and the mechanic Saager climbed into the vehicle belonging to local Sheriff Lillian Holley's and fled the area.

The most notorious prisoner in the country had escaped from the escape-proof prison without a single shot being fired. After getting out of town, Dillinger ordered the vehicle to stop. He handed Saager four dollars so the pair could return to town.

Dillinger then apologized that he didn't have more to spare.

Unfortunately, Dillinger had unknowingly committed a federal crime: crossing state lines with a stolen vehicle. This act drew the attention of the FBI, and so Dillinger had quickly become one of the most wanted men in the world.

By the summer of 1934, John Dillinger had disappeared from view. Due to his notoriety, Dillinger's life had become increasingly difficult. On Dillinger's birthday, June 22, the FBI had declared him America's first "Public Enemy No. 1" and placed a $10,000 reward on his head.

In order to avoid detection, Dillinger

underwent plastic surgery on his face to alter his distinguishing features. Dillinger evaded detection for several more months, but the FBI had set up a dedicated task force in order to locate him.

Dillinger was apprehended by the FBI on July 22nd, 1934 outside a theatre in Chicago. A shoot-out between Dillinger and the FBI quickly ensued, resulting in Dillinger's death. He was 31 years old.

Dillinger's life can be considered by many to be the embodiment of the word "short". He was a man of impulse and quick thinking. Throughout his short life he went through more friends, girlfriends, relationships and acquaintances, homes and criminal activity than most people do in a full lifetime. His life was categorized by single-serving incidents which fulfilled a short-term requirement.

John Dillinger's final prison escape is by far the most remarkable thing to his name. The fact he was able to escape a maximum-security jail with nothing but a fake gun is a testament to his ferocity and his fearlessness. This act has inspired similar incidents over the years, with people using inanimate objects as illusions of weaponry.

As with many notorious gangsters, John Dillinger received somewhat celebrity status during his final years, and particularly in the modern world where his crimes have become something of legend. The impact John Dillinger has had in regards to the archetypal image of an American gangster

cannot be understated, and he has left a
legacy of surreal incidents in his wake.

Brian Bo Larsen – The Record-Holding Prison Escapist

While escaping from prison is not necessarily a positive thing, it can indeed be considered an achievement. As with any feat which can be accurately quantified, there will always be a record-holder. The record holder in this case is a little-known Danish criminal named Brian Bo Larsen – a man who has escaped prison 22 times.

It was perhaps in Brian Bo Larsen's childhood that the notion of escaping became a constant in his life. Larsen's childhood was rife with criminal activity and violent incidents. It began with his father's abuse during his adolescent years which progressed regularly into severe canings and out-right physical assault. His father was an alcoholic who was unable to control his anger, and Larsen would often take the punishments in favor of his mother.

His real criminal activity began at the age of eight. While other children were busy playing with dinosaur toys and video games, Brian Bo Larsen was stealing things from shops in order to survive. His neglect at the hands of his parents forced him to go long periods without food and forced him to wear the same unwashed clothes each day for school. This turned him onto a crime spree which continued right through into adulthood.

While he was not considered to be intellectually-challenged in any means, his violent upbringing made him unable to connect with the other children in his classes. He would steal toys and sweets from the other children. Robbery became his go-to source to acquire anything he needed; a response triggered by his primal instinct to survive.

It was at the age of thirteen which Larsen committed his first serious offence. Larsen approached the cashier at a local service station and threatened the cashier with a large knife he had stolen from another store. The cashier was made to hand over cigarettes and alcohol, which Larsen took along with a large quantity of food. Unfortunately for Larsen, he was caught quite clearly on the station's CCTV footage and the police began the hunt for him.

Even by the age of thirteen, Brian Bo Larsen was known to authorities as a trouble-maker. It didn't take them long to track Larsen down as his whereabouts were common knowledge to the police and so he was quickly apprehended.

Due to the obvious neglect which Larsen suffered at the hands of his parents, Larsen wasn't sent to any kind of correctional facility and was instead placed in a foster home with hopes that he could reform. Unfortunately, Larsen's state of mind appeared to be beyond repair by any foster parents, and was subsequently sent across multiple foster homes. He eventually ended up In Lohals foster home in Langeland, Denmark.

The idyllic village appeared to be a place where Larsen may be able to eventually subside from his criminal activity and recover, but unfortunately this was not the case. At his new school, Larsen emptied the school safe of money on not one but two occasions. This would be the final straw for authorities, who then sentenced Larsen to community service so he could earn the money to repay the school.

In 1989, at the age of sixteen, Larsen received his first jail sentence. Larsen had been caught stealing petrol from a local garage in order to sell on for profit. Unfortunately, the garage owner caught him on CCTV and pressed charges. Larsen was sent to Ungdomsinstitutionen Egely facility in Funen, Denmark. It would be here that Larsen would make his first escape from jail.

For his first escape, Larsen simply dug a tunnel beneath his cell over the course of his imprisonment. Similar to the infamous Alcatraz escapees, there was a vent which Larsen used for leverage. The ready-made hole, despite it being very small, offered a starting point for him to begin digging through. Using materials found throughout the prison, Larsen extended this hole far enough to reach the outside of the prison, resulting in his eventual escape.

What soon became apparent to Larsen is that remaining a fugitive is harder than it seems.

In less than a year, Larsen was re-captured by Danish authorities and sent to Nyborg State Prison in Statsfaengsel, Denmark.

There, Larsen employed a similar tactic to escape but with an added twist. A vent large enough to pass a person through was housed in the corridor outside of Larsen's cell. Larsen obtained a screwdriver from another inmate, removed the screws from the vent and escaped through it in a short enough time that the guards never even saw it happen.

For the next few years, Larsen was in and out of multiple facilities across Denmark for different crimes, most of which involved robbery. In 1992, he served four separate stints across three jails (Sikrede Institution,

Statsfaengslet, and Arresthuset), escaping all of them a total of four times. In just three years of imprisonment, Brian Bo Larsen had escaped six times from five different facilities.

His actions became incredibly concerning to the Danish government. Not only was this man proving to be uncapturable, he was also making a mockery of the Danish legal system. He was served two more stints the following year in state prisons in Horsens and Ringe, and true to his history, he escaped both of them with relative ease.

In 1994, Larsen committed his most serious offence to date. He committed armed robbery of convenience store and stole the equivalent of around $6000 in cash. In 1995,

He was sent to state prison in Vridsloselille, a place he would eventually break out of a total of four times.

His first stint saw him escape via a stroke of luck when a large truck veered off-course and crashed into the prison wall while Larsen was in the courtyard. Although there were many inmates there at the time, Larsen was the only one to make a successful escape.

In the year 2000, Larsen was imprisoned in three further different facilities across Denmark (Kolding Arresthus, Svendborg Politigard, and Svendborg Arresthus) as his constant escapism was now being seen as something akin to supernatural ability. As if to prove this theory, Larsen escaped all of them with progressing surrealism.

On one occasion, Larsen buried himself in dirt during his admittance to a prison courtyard. When all other inmates were sent back to their cells and guards had returned to their posts, Larsen used his isolation to climb over the prison walls to freedom. On another occasion, he dug a tunnel underneath the courtyard to the other side of the prison walls.

In 2004, Larsen committed perhaps his most bizarre escape while he was on sweeping duty. His job was to collect all of the leaves in the prison courtyard and place them in large containers. For the final container, Larsen climbed in the container himself just as they were about to be sent out via lorry.

When the driver of the vehicle stopped to empty all of the containers, Larsen jumped out and escaped to freedom.

Most recently, Larsen escaped Vridsloseselille State Prison just outside Copenhagen by sawing the bars off his cell window with a hacksaw. He then used a rope ladder to climb to the top of the roof, then another to climb back down to freedom.

Despite his record-breaking amount of escapes, Brian Bo Larsen has spent more than half his life behind bars. Now aged 43 years old in 2017, there is a significant chance that he will spend the remainder of his life being admitted to and thusly escaping from various facilities across Denmark, perhaps even from other countries too.

Larsen's current status as of 2017 is incarcerated in Statsfaengslet, Vridsloseselille; the same place he broke out of in 2014.

After escaping in 2014, Larsen fled and remained free for several months, but was eventually tracked down on Funen Island after he had wrecked a stolen car while high on drugs. He was discovered with a sex worker who claims that Larsen crashed through a fence while he was hallucinating and started to have imaginary fights with people.

There is very little information on Brian Bo Larsen which has been translated to English, despite his incredible life. His status in Denmark is somewhat of a celebrity-trickster, although there is little knowledge of him to be obtained outside of his home country.

The fact that Brian Bo Larsen has escaped prison a record amount of times is incredible by itself. However, what make his escapes truly amazing is the ingenious methods which he has employed to escape. Some of his tactics would even seem too far-fetched for fiction. Just as incredible is that not only has Brian Bo Larsen escaped jail so many times, it's that he's also escaped from different locations; holding pens, lock-ups, maximum-security centers and juvenile facilities. It seems that there is no cell in the world unable to keep Brian Bo Larsen contained.

Just how Brian Bo Larsen manages to continue to evade jail so seamlessly is indicative of his creativity. While it is true that Danish prisons are much more lax in comparison to American and British prisons, their jails are still designed to keep prisoners contained. If Danish prisons were significantly easier to escape than other parts of the world, there would be a lot more jail breaks in Denmark. However, Brian Bo Larsen appears to be a unique figure in criminal history.

In 2012, T.J. Lane became a name known across the world when he carried out a school shooting at Chardon High School in Chardon, Ohio. Only seventeen years of age,

T.J. Lane shot and killed three fellow students on February 27th.

Lane began his shooting spree at 7:30am on a Monday morning. He walked into Chardon High School cafeteria and began shooting a .22 calibre pistol at students who were still eating breakfast.

Lane managed to fatally wound three students and leave another three wounded before he was chased out of the school by a teacher. Lane was only outside of the school for a brief moment before being restrained and arrested by authorities.

As is the case with most school shootings, the culprits are usually juvenile delinquents suffering with severe mental anguish. They are often not the most straight-thinking of individuals, despite their in-depth planning of their attacks. They are usually encumbered with thoughts of revenge and violence and forego rational thinking in favor of planning out their fantasies.

This is what makes the fact that T.J. Lane was able to escape from prison such an interesting feat.

Indeed, Lane fit this profile of a juvenile delinquent perfectly. Lane's childhood was a constant barrage of abuse and neglect from his parents. His father in particular had a history of domestic violence against women, resulting in his severe abuse of Lane's mother. His arrest history was substantial, and likely indicates regular violence against his son in addition to beating his wife.

When Lane was in his early teenage years, he was sent to live with his grandparents. This is common amongst violent parents who cannot adequately care for their children; however, it can create an unhealthy mental state for the child. It creates a feeling of worthlessness and unimportance, which the unconscious mind desperately tries to compensate for.

In the case of T.J. Lane, he attempted to get revenge on a world he felt he didn't belong to. He did this by murdering people he saw as more privileged than he was. Something which passed by the radar of the media during the time of Lane's shooting was that Lane didn't even attend the Chardon School that he attacked. He was actually a student at Lake Academy in nearby Willoughby, which is an alternative school for at-risk youth, many of whom have struggled with addiction or suffered abuse at home.

On September 11th 2014, T.J. Lane escaped from the unit he was due to serve three life sentences in: Allen Correctional Institution in Lima, Ohio. Lane had previously been disciplined by authorities at the institution a total of seven times already by the time of his escape. His infractions ranged from urinating up walls inside the prison, tattooing himself and refusing to follow the orders of prison officials.

During recreational hours, Lane and two other inmates used a ladder they had crudely fashioned out of cabinets to scale the prison fence, resulting in their escape. The two other inmates; 33 year old Lindsey Bruce and 45 year old Clifford Opperud – both of whom were doing time for aggravated burglary, were soon discovered by authorities in the surrounding area. However, Lane evaded capture for significantly longer.

The group fashioned their "ladder" over several months from materials they discovered inside a crawlspace located nearby to the recreation yard. The door to the crawlspace was sufficiently padlocked, but the inmates were able to break their way in regardless.

On the day of their jail break, they used the

ladder to get on top of a building near the prison entrance at around 7:40pm. They then jumped around 15 feet down to the ground and escaped through a soybean field.

Authorities believed Lane to be "potentially armed and dangerous", which, given Lane's unpredictable mental state, was very likely to be the case. Residents in the surrounding areas were advised to lock their doors and stay inside their homes as Lane would likely be looking for somewhere to hide out. It would be not be a stretch to assume he would easily force his way into a person's home given his history of violence.

As a safety precaution, Chardon High School was closed the same day for fear of Lane returning to finish what he began two years previous. His escape caused outrage amongst the parents and residents of the Chardon area, particularly the parents with children Lane had taken the lives of. To be so careless in their supervision of such a notorious offender was seen as an insult to everyone affected by his actions.

Fortunately, T.J. Lane was re-captured the following morning. He was found only 100 yards away from the prison he escaped from in a wooded area. Lane did reportedly not put up any kind of resistance when apprehended for the second time, nor did he say a word.

The same day he was returned, T.J. Lane was transferred to Ohio State Penitentiary, a maximum security prison in Ohio. As of

2016, Lane now resides in Southern Ohio Correctional Facility; the most secure jail in the state. It is very unlikely Lane will ever leave this unit, and will serve his three life sentences under the watchful eye of the highest security protocols possible.

T.J. Lane was nineteen at the time of his jail break. As of 2017, he remains the youngest person to ever escape a state prison.

Conclusion

For as long as we have prisons, we will have those who escape them.

Despite their mythical allure and their Hollywood-inspiring dramatizations, it is important to remember that a prison escape usually means that a dangerous criminal is back on the streets.

Real life crime isn't as romanticized as it is in the movies. Most prison breaks usually aren't carried out by suave masterminds in suits and expensive suede shoes, but rather impulsive, desperate, immoral criminals who have been apprehended by the law for good reason.

Over time, we come to forget that this is the case. Historical criminals such as John Dillinger and the Alcatraz prisoners come to be seen as heroes for their complete disregard for society's rules. It is easy to forget that they are deplorable beings who *belong* behind bars, despite stories of their bid for freedoms being as fascinating and awe-inspiring as they are.

Popular culture has a long connection with prison breaks, as can be seen by the amount of dramatizations of famous escapes. Indeed, at least three of the famous cases in this volume have been translated to film or TV, often with a fabricated narrative regarding each criminal's actual reasons for being imprisoned.

To escape jail requires a determination to break the rules and live a life free of consequences. It requires a combination of extreme manipulation, outside accomplices, bribed authorities, excessive planning and sometimes, just dumb luck.

Regardless, no matter where prison breaks fall on the spectrum of morality, there's no denying their fascination.

CPSIA information can be obtained
at www.ICGtesting.com
Printed in the USA
BVHW040529140223
658474BV00017B/196

9 781521 591208